JOYS
OF
CHRISTMAS

This book
is for everyone who loves
the sounds and smells
and sights of
Christmas.

The Joys of Christmas

Christmas Customs and Legends Around the World

by
Kathryn Jackson

illustrated by
Jenny Williams

gb GOLDEN PRESS • NEW YORK

Western Publishing Company, Inc., Racine, Wisconsin

Counting the Days Till Christmas

December is here.

And suddenly, it's as if some mysterious cupboard, crammed full of the sights and sounds and smells of Christmas, were thrown open.

One by one, out come the old customs and legends—handed down from grandparents to parents and from country to country—that make Christmas all that it is today. The first customs to spill out, three ways of counting off the days until Christmas, come from Germany.

Some families set up a three-fold Advent Calendar December first. They open one of its small, numbered doors each day until Advent ends—on Christmas Eve.

Other families make an Advent Wreath of evergreens with four fat candles fastened firmly in it. On the first Sunday in Advent, they light one candle. On the second Sunday, they light two candles, and so on. And each day of the Advent season, they add a gilt-paper star to their wreath.

Still other families take out their treasured Star of Seven, a seven-branched candlestick. They set one candle alight on the first Sunday in December, two more each Sunday thereafter.

Around Advent Calendar, Wreath, or Star of Seven, the family gathers to hear the story of the First Christmas, sing favorite carols, and plan the secret surprises they want to give, or find under their tree, on Christmas Day.

7

Christmas Markets

It's the custom in Old Nuremberg, in Germany, to open the huge outdoor Christmas Market in early December.

To the sound of carol singers, hawkers crying their wares, and sometimes a lively marching band, the shoppers go from one brightly decorated stall to another. They can look at charming wooden toys from the toymakers in the Black Forest, mechanical toys from Germany's many toy factories, toys of all kinds from places all around the world.

Frosted gingerbread figures, figures of sugary marzipan, and delicately-made glass ornaments twinkle and beckon through the soft-falling snow as well. It's hard to choose from that exciting array!

But Christmas shopping takes time everywhere—in big city stores and shops, and in tiny village markets all around the world.

In Germany, people greet one another with *"Froehliche Weihnachten!"* at Christmas time.

And Christmas Wares

Each country has its own special wares to sell at Christmas time.

France is known for beautiful dolls, and a cake shaped like a Yule log, with chocolate frosting. In Sweden, there are small figures of the *Jultomten,* a merry Christmas elf, and Christmas is not complete without a *Julbukk,* a straw goat, for good luck.

Mexico has brightly painted tin toys, and small clay animals and people to add to miniature manger scenes. Ireland must have plenty of candles to sell, for here people light every window on Christmas Eve to guide the Christ Child on His way.

And in the United States, besides toys and gifts from around the world, there are figures of Santa Claus—in all sizes and materials—smiling from every shop window.

| Gustav has chosen a droll, carved nutcracker from the Christmas Market in Old Nuremberg. | In a big store in Paris, Amalie has found the doll she hopes *le Père Noël* will bring her. | And in Mexico, Miguel can't quite decide between a fat clay *piñata,* and a small, live burro. |

Christmas Letters, Cards–and Stamps

It's the custom to write a letter to Santa Claus, *le Père Noël,* Kriss Kringle, or Father Christmas. Or—if you live in a country where the Three Kings bring toys to the boys and girls—to write to them.

Some letters are burned, and the wind blows the ashes, and your wishes, where you want them to go. Some letters are left on a windowsill, to be picked up by special Christmas helpers.

And some are mailed, with real Christmas stamps.

Christmas cards, the kind you buy, were first printed in England about one hundred years ago. By now, the custom of sending greeting cards to friends has spread around the world.

The idea of Christmas seals, sold to help others, was first thought of by a post office clerk in Denmark.

10

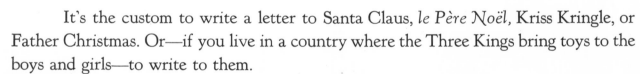

People in Denmark greet one another with "*Glaedelig Jul!*"

Christmas Wrappings

No one knows when, or where, the custom of wrapping Christmas gifts began. Perhaps it was in Denmark, where every package must be wrapped so no one can possibly guess what's inside.

A pair of earrings may be wrapped in so many layers that the package is as big as a bass drum. A book may look like a ball, a doll like a star—and a wagon like nothing you've ever seen!

There may be a different name on each layer of paper, so that the package keeps changing hands. Or there may be no gift inside—but a card giving a clue to where your gift is hidden.

There's no end to the trouble some Danish families will take in wrapping their gifts to make opening —or finding—them more exciting.

In Denmark, these disguised gifts are called *Julklapp*.

11

St. Nicholas Eve-and Day

In Belgium and the Netherlands, the Christmas season begins on December fifth—St. Nicholas Eve.

Good St. Nicholas makes a short visit to every home to ask which children were good all year—which not so good. It seems that no one can fool him, for as he leaves the door is left open and a fresh white sheet is spread before it. And soon, in comes a shower of candies, or—sometimes—only a handful of switches!

The next day, St. Nicholas—gorgeously dressed and on a white horse—rides through town. The children are out in swarms and bevies to wave to him or shake hands. And to keep an eye on his companion, Black Peter, who makes a list of those who may not deserve any presents this year.

12

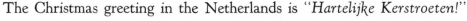

The Christmas greeting in the Netherlands is "*Hartelijke Kerstroeten!*"

St. Lucia's Day

December thirteenth is *Luciadagen,* or St. Lucy's Day, in Sweden.

Early in the morning, the oldest daughter of the house takes a tray of coffee and sweet buns up to her parents. She wears a white gown, a scarlet sash, and a crown of greens. Her sisters and brothers, all in white, follow her. The boys, in their tall pointed caps, are her Star Boys for this one day.

In many towns, a St. Lucia is chosen to carry the coffee and buns to each home. Her followers carry candles and sing carols as they walk through the snowy darkness of morning in Sweden.

St. Lucia's Day is celebrated in Italy, too, for she is a favorite saint. But here, it's the custom to light huge bonfires in her honor, and to have lovely candlelight processions in the evening.

In Sweden, the Christmas greeting is "*Gud Jul!*"

13

A Crèche for Christmas

The first manger scene was set up in Italy, by Francis of Assisi, the patron saint of animals. It was life-sized, with real animals gathered around the Babe—and all the figures dressed in gorgeous cloth.

Later, people in Southern Europe began to set up miniature manger scenes in their homes. In France, the children often decide where their *crèche* will be placed.

One by one, they take each small figure from a storage box, carefully unwrap it, and set it in the stable. They may save *le Petit Noël*, the exquisite figure of the Christ Child, for last. From then till Christmas, the family will gather at their *crèche* to sing carols. And to think about that wondrous night, so long ago, when *le Petit Noël* was born.

14

At Christmas time in France, people wish one another "*Joyeux Noël!*"

Animals at Christmas

The animals, perhaps because they drew near the manger on the First Christmas, have an important part in legends and customs.

One old legend tells that the animals kneel at midnight on Christmas Eve. Another, that at that same hour, they are given the gift of speech—and that it is bad luck for anyone to listen to their words.

In Norway, Sweden, and Denmark, families put out a sheaf of grain for the wild birds at Christmas time. In these countries, too, it's said that the Christmas elves will torment any farmer who has neglected his animals at any time during the year.

And in Portugal and Brazil, the first church service on Christmas morning is called *Missa do Gallo*. It was named for the rooster that crows at dawn.

People in Norway call out "*Gledelig Jul!*" at Christmas time.

Bringing Christmas Home

Decking homes with greens is an old Christmas custom. Long, long ago, it was believed that bringing in garlands of fresh greens might entice the woodland sprites into the house, too, to bring good cheer.

Even today, children in England go out hunting for holly, ivy, and mistletoe to bring home.

Holly was once thought of as belonging to Mary, its bright berries standing for warm, womanly ways. Ivy was thought of as standing for merrymaking. And a young man might kiss a girl under the mistletoe—but only if he gave her a berry for every kiss.

Rosemary—for friendship—and other sweet-smelling herbs, were once Christmas greens. Some families still use them in their Christmas decorations.

16

The English Christmas greeting is "Happy Christmas!"

The Yule Log

The Yule log blazing on the hearth is said to bring Christmas light, joy, and good luck—especially in northern countries where the winter is cold, long, and dark much of the day.

In Provence, France, a huge log is brought in by the family—the youngest walking last in line. Around the kitchen they go once, twice, thrice, before putting it on the hearth.

The father pours a little wine on the log and says:

"Joy, joy, joy upon us, for Christmas brings all good things!"

"Joy, joy, joy!" the children chorus.

As the father lights the fire, he says, "Burn the Yule log, oh fire!"

Then he and all his family stand back to watch it flame and fill their kitchen with its warm Christmas light.

Provence, like all of France, uses the greeting "*Joyeux Noël!*"

17

Christmas Pageants and Pantomime

Around the world, it's time to practice for the Christmas pageant. Fathers hammer away at scenery. Mothers work on robes, wings, and halos—for in many countries the pageant will be about the Christ Child's birth on the first Christmas.

In England, troops of actors are ready to put on the Christmas Pantomime—a hodgepodge of fairy tale, nursery rhyme, and hilarious nonsense. Ballet companies around the world are perfecting the *Nutcracker Suite,* the beloved Christmas story that was written in Germany.

In Russia, there will be performances of the Legend of Babouschka and in Denmark, of a story by her own Hans Christian Andersen.

And in France, girls and boys are quite sure they will be taken to a puppet show—as part of their Christmas treat.

The Christmas greeting in Russia is "*Hristos Razdajetsja!*"

A Christmas Procession

Not long before Christmas, every town in Mexico has a nightly candlelight procession called *Las Posadas,* an acting out of the search for shelter in Bethlehem.

Two children, carrying small clay figures of Joseph and Mary, lead the others to the home chosen as the first *posada.* Here they stop and sing a little song begging to come in and rest.

The hosts, singing too, tell them to be on their way.

But when the song tells that it is Joseph and Mary seeking shelter, the group is invited in to rest, eat, and sing around the *nacimiento*—the manger scene in the Mexican home.

Last of all, the children break open a large clay *piñata* filled with candies and surprises—and everyone scrambles for his share.

19

The Mexican Christmas greeting is "*¡Felices Pascuas*"

O Christmas Tree!

The Christmas tree comes to us from Germany.

There are many beautiful legends about its origin.

One tells that on the first Christmas Eve, the winter trees bloomed as if it were springtime.

Another legend says that Martin Luther, the stern reformer, lighted candles on a small fir tree to show his little son how the starry heavens must have looked on that first silent Christmas Eve.

Still another legend tells of a wandering child who was taken into the home of a poor forester, fed, and tucked into a warm bed. In the morning, the child was seen to be the Christ Child Himself.

Before He left the humble cottage, He put an evergreen twig in the ground and promised that it would grow to be a tall tree that would—ever after—bring plenty to the forester and his family.

20

The German song "*O Tannenbaum!*" honors the Christmas tree.

Bright Lights and Ornaments

Over the years, people have found many ways of making their Christmas trees bloom with dazzling beauty.

Candles, or lights, stand for the joy and light of Christmas.

Shiny paper hearts and cornucopias filled with candy stand for the happiness of giving generously to others. The garlands of tiny flags used in Scandinavia stand for love of country. Small animals (of tin in Mexico, straw or thin wood in Scandinavia, and of delicate, shimmering blown glass in Germany) remind people of the animals at the manger.

Candy canes stand for the crooks the shepherds used.

And the shining star at the top of every tree stands for the bright star of wondrous size that shone—a long, long time ago—above the silent stable in Bethlehem.

21

The earliest Christmas trees were trimmed with real fruit and flowers.

Christmas Stockings

The custom of hanging stockings on Christmas Eve stems from an old legend. It is said that St. Nicholas, then a kindly Greek bishop, took pity on a poor man whose three comely daughters could not marry because he had no gold for their dowries.

By night, the good bishop dropped a purse full of gold down the man's chimney. It landed, by chance, in one of the stockings the eldest daughter had hung up to dry. Now she could be married.

Soon the next daughter, then the next, hung up a stocking for St. Nicholas to fill with gold.

He did and, in turn, they were married to good men, too.

In time, because of this legend, children began hanging up their stockings—hoping to find them filled with gifts.

22

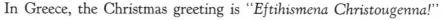

In Greece, the Christmas greeting is *"Eftihismena Christougenna!"*

And Shoes to be Filled with Gifts

In many countries, children don't hang up stockings.

They put their shoes out instead.

Dutch and Belgian children once put out their big wooden shoes, or *sabots,* for the Christ Child to fill. Today, they may put out *sabots* or their regular shoes.

In Spain, Mexico, Puerto Rico, and many South American countries—where it is the custom for the Three Kings to bring gifts—boys and girls fill their shoes with hay for the Kings' camels, and put them on their windowsills.

There are places, too, where each child in a family puts out an empty basket or plate and—in the morning—finds it filled with candies, small toys, and other tiny and wonderful surprises.

23

People who speak Spanish greet one another with "*¡Felices Pascuas*"

The Music of Christmas

Music has always brought its own kind of joy to Christmas.

The Christmas Story tells of angels singing above the stable in Bethlehem. Long ago in Italy, shepherds came down from the hills to pipe their sweetest *pastorales* in the slow-gathering night of Christmas Eve.

Later on, the English waits—town musicians—went from house to house singing and playing "Away in a Manger," or bidding householders "Deck the halls with boughs of holly—Fa-la-la-la-la, la-la, la-la!"

The gentle carol "Silent Night" came from Germany, the lilting "Little Drummer Boy" from Spain. "Good King Wenceslaus" was written about a kindly king of old Bohemia. Today, these carols are sung in so many countries that they seem to weave a wreath of joyful song all around the world throughout the Christmas season.

24

The Christmas greeting in Italy is *"Buon Natale!"*

Christmas Bells

Bells ring out on city streets, and carillons ring out from high in village steeples. Tiny bells tinkle mysteriously as people tie them on their Christmas packages.

But once, a long time ago in England, all the bells were silent.

It was forbidden to celebrate Christmas at all.

The monks at Whitby Abbey were ordered to sell the abbey bells—the sacred bells which had long rung out from their bell tower.

While the bells were on their way to London, the ship that carried them sank. But the townspeople said that, each year on Christmas Eve, they heard the bells ring out—from beneath the deep, dark waves.

To this day, bells ring out at Christmas time.

Many children fall asleep on Christmas Eve waiting—and straining their ears—to hear the faraway jingling of the bells on Santa Claus' sleigh.

25

Bells, big and small, have their own way of saying *"Merry Christmas!"*

Santa Claus and His Reindeer

In many countries, Santa Claus will soon be coming down from the North Pole with his sleigh loaded with wonderful toys.

It's hard to believe that this jolly sprite, looking just as he does today, first appeared only a century and a half ago. It was then that Clement Moore wrote a poem about Santa and his eight little reindeer, and the magical way he comes down the chimney with his enormous pack full of toys. Next, the artist Thomas Nast drew pictures of him, and of his helpers, for a newspaper.

Being magical—the spirit of gift-giving—Santa Claus gets in even when there is no chimney. There's no doubt about that, for every Christmas morning children in the United States and many other countries find his presents under their shining trees.

26

People in the United States say "*Merry Christmas!*" to one another.

More Christmas Visitors

Santa Claus, though he travels far, isn't the only spirit of Christmas gift-giving.

By no means.

In France, it is *Père Noël,* or sometimes *le Petit Noël,* who brings toys to boys and girls. The *Christkind* showers presents on Dutch and Belgian children—those who get a good report from St. Nicholas and watchful Black Peter.

English children are given their toys by jolly, old Father Christmas.

Swedish children dream of presents from the little *Jultomten,* an elf with a long beard. German children wait for a visit, on Christmas Eve, from Kriss Kringle.

And in Finland, Old Man Christmas—once a jolly goat all dressed in red—comes down from Lapland with a great sack all full of Christmas toys.

27

The Christmas greeting in Finland is "*Hauskaa Joulua!*"

Waiting for Little Christmas Eve

Just as there are different Christmas visitors around the world, there are different days for the big celebration.

In Denmark on December twenty-second, the children are sniffing and peeking, and waiting for tomorrow—Little Christmas Eve. Tomorrow they will feast on roast goose, lucky rice pudding, and the Christmas fish and breads and cookies that their mothers are so busily, and happily, making.

Tomorrow the door to the main room will be thrown open upon a tall tree decked with tinsel, tiny Danish flags, paper hearts filled with candies, and lighted—not with strings of colored bulbs—with dozens of real candles.

And tomorrow in Denmark, the little *Julnisse*—first cousin to the Swedish *Jultomten*—will come hurrying in with his bag full of toys to give to all the waiting round-eyed boys and girls.

In Denmark, the Christmas rice pudding is called *risengrød*.

Waiting for Christmas Eve

Children in Germany wait eagerly for Christmas Eve, which is their big day of feasting, surprises, and Christmas joy. They won't be sent early to bed. Instead, they'll be allowed to stay up long, long after the splendid holiday feast.

In some homes, once the feast is over, the grandfather will get out his small Christmas Eve drum. Beating merrily on it, he'll lead a march all through the house. The family, from biggest to smallest, will follow him upstairs and down, along halls and around corners, to the locked door of the Christmas Tree Room.

Grandfather will open the door on the dazzling sight of the fragrant fir tree. The family will march round and round it, singing carols and eyeing the gifts heaped high under its branches.

When "*Stille Nacht*," the last carol has been sung—and the last of the packages has been opened—it will be nearly midnight.

29

"*Stille Nacht*" is the German name for the lovely carol "Silent Night."

And Waiting for Christmas Day–Itself

Christmas Day is celebrated in many, many countries and in many ways.

In the United States, the children will creep out of their beds at first light to find their stockings bulging with surprises.

They'll stand, hearts thumping, looking up at the shining Christmas tree with packages—and toys from Santa—around it.

And then, suddenly, the noise and excitement of Christmas will begin.

Toys will be tried out, packages opened, greetings and hugs exchanged. The phone will start ringing more Merry Christmases. Someone will turn on soft Christmas carols. Someone will hurry to light the Christmas logs.

Outside, snow may be falling in great, white feathery flakes. And from near and far, all over city or town, the bells will ring out the joyful news that Christmas Day is here—at last.

Merry Christmas!   Froehliche Weihnachten!   Joyeux Noël!   Glaedelig Jul!

Here, and around the world, many people will go to church.

Then they may hurry out, carrying armloads of presents to relatives and friends—and shut-ins—who live nearby.

And then, in homes crowded with grandparents, aunts and uncles, and dozens of cousins, it will be time for the Christmas feast. Will it be turkey, roast beef, goose, or whole roast pig? Will there be mince pie, plum pudding, or a richly frosted Yule log cake?

Will Santa Claus, *Père Noël, Jultomten* or *Julnisse*—or a single, shining star—brighten the evergreens in the centerpiece?

It all depends on the customs that grandparents—or great-grandparents, or great-great-grandparents—brought from a faraway country in a time long ago, but never forgotten at Christmas time.

31

Eftihismena Christougenna!   Hartelijke Kerstroeten!   Happy Christmas!   Hauskaa Joulua!

Bright Days After Christmas

The joys of Christmas don't end with Christmas Day.

Nor does the marvelous old carved cupboard, filled with Christmas customs and legends, close its doors with a magical *click!*

On Three Kings' Day, January sixth, children in Spain, Mexico, Puerto Rico, and many South American countries will find their shoes filled with sweets. Their presents will be heaped alongside. And since the hay the children left for the Three Kings' camels is always gone—there can be no doubt about who brought their presents.

On Epiphany—the sixth of January, too—children in Northern Europe will find their presents from *le Petit Noël,* or the *Christkind,* or Kriss Kringle, or sometimes from Santa Claus.

In Italy, it is the good fairy, *Befana,* who brings presents to all good children.

And in Russia, it is *Babouschka*—poor old Babouschka, who was once too busy to help the Three Kings on their way to Bethlehem—who still wanders about bringing gifts to the children.

It is said that, as she trudges through the deep snow, she keeps hoping to find the little Christ Child fast asleep in one of the many quiet houses she visits on the Eve of Three Kings' Day.

Gud Jul!   Buon Natale!   ¡Felices Pascuas   Hristos Razdajetsja!

33